First published 1987 by Walker Books Ltd
184-192 Drummond Street, London NW1 3HP

First printed 1987
Printed and bound by L.E.G.O., Vicenza, Italy

British Library Cataloguing in Publication Data
Hayes, Sarah
Away in a manger.
1. Jesus Christ – Nativity –
Juvenile literature
I. Title   II. Moore, Inga
232.9′21   BT315.2

ISBN 0-7445-0676-X

AWAY IN A MANGER

Story by Sarah Hayes
Pictures by Inga Moore

WALKER BOOKS
LONDON

CONTENTS

THE STORY BEGINS

Long ago, in the city of Nazareth, a young woman sat sewing in a courtyard. She loved to be outside in the cool of the evening after the fierce heat of the midday sun. The woman's name was Mary, and she was soon to be married to a man called Joseph. There was much to do before the wedding and her fingers flew at her work.

Suddenly Mary heard a noise and she looked up. For a moment she thought the courtyard was on fire. Then, in the centre of the brightness, she saw an angel. The angel was smiling, but Mary was afraid, and she hid her face in her hands.

"Do not be afraid," said the angel, "for you have been chosen by God to bear his son. In a few months your baby will be born, and his name will be Jesus."

THE DONKEY'S STORY

The old grey donkey stood in the middle of the field watching the men talking by the fence. One was her master, but the other man was a stranger.

"We have to leave Nazareth today," she heard the stranger say. "The Romans are counting the people in our country, and I have been ordered to register in Bethlehem, where I was born. I need a donkey who will carry my wife to Bethlehem."

The old grey donkey nibbled the dry grass and did not look up. She knew that the stranger would not be interested in her. There were other donkeys in the field much younger and stronger than she.

"What about that grey one in the middle of the field?" said a new voice. The grey donkey looked up and saw a young woman dressed in blue who came forward and put out her hand. So gentle was her voice and so sweet her smile that the grey donkey walked up and began to nuzzle the woman's palm.

"She's never done that to anyone but me," said the donkey seller. "This lady must be someone very special."

And so she was, for the woman's name was Mary and the stranger's name was Joseph.

"Look, sir," said the donkey seller, "you can take my grey. I'll give her to you. She's nearly too old for service, but she'll take you to Bethlehem all right. She should know the way."

It was many miles from Nazareth to Bethlehem, but the old grey donkey never stumbled.

If there were sharp stones on the road, she took care to avoid them. And if she heard snakes or lizards rustling in the grass, she walked straight past them.

On the fourth day the old grey donkey plodded into Bethlehem. Night was coming and the air was getting cold. Joseph was anxious to find somewhere to stay for he knew that Mary's baby would soon be born. But everywhere they asked, the answer was the same: there were no rooms to be had. Eventually the weary donkey brought Joseph and Mary to an inn on the far side of the city. As Joseph knocked, a shuttered window was flung open and a red face looked out.

"There is no room at the inn," said the red-faced man, closing the shutters firmly. Then the window opened again. "But seeing as you won't get a room anywhere else," said the innkeeper, "you could have my stable. It's clean and it's dry. But it's only a stable."

"A stable will do for us," said Joseph.

The innkeeper led the way across the yard to the stable. The grey donkey could hear the ox moving in his stall and she could smell the new hay in the manger. But she was aware of something else, something strangely familiar. Without knowing it, the donkey had brought Mary and Joseph to the stable where she had been born many years before.

After all her travels, the old grey donkey had come home.

LITTLE DONKEY

Little donkey, little donkey,
On the dusty road.
Got to keep on plodding onwards,
With your precious load.
Been a long time, little donkey,
Thro' the winter's night.
Don't give up now, little donkey,
Bethlehem's in sight.

Ring out those bells tonight,
Bethlehem, Bethlehem.
Follow that star tonight,
Bethlehem, Bethlehem.
Little donkey, little donkey,
Had a heavy day.
Little donkey, carry Mary
Safely on her way.

Little donkey, little donkey,
Journey's end is near.
There are wise men, waiting for
A sign to bring them here.
Do not falter, little donkey,
There's a star ahead.
It will guide you, little donkey,
To a cattle shed.

chorus

THE OX'S STORY

In the stable the ox tried to see what was happening. He knew there were strangers in the barn. But who they were and what they were doing in his stable, he could not imagine.

Then came the familiar sound of the innkeeper's steps on the straw and an old grey donkey was pushed into the ox's stall.

"You've got company tonight," the innkeeper said. "And so have we. More than enough." He was not a harsh master, but his manners were rough. The ox and the innkeeper understood each other very well.

The ox moved aside to let the grey donkey feed from the manger, but she was too tired to eat. In a while she slept.

As the night wore on, the ox's eyes closed once or twice, but he did not sleep much. It was not his way. It was enough to be still, not pulling the heavy cart laden with food for the inn, or dragging the plough across the dry earth. The ox listened to the two voices rising and falling, one soft and anxious, the other deep and reassuring.

Then, through the darkness, the ox heard a new sound: the tiny wail of a newborn baby.

"He shall be called Jesus," the ox heard the soft voice say. And then there was silence.

After a moment the ox was surprised to see a man's face peering into his manger. Watching him pat down the hay, the ox noticed that the man's hands were rough and scarred. He could not know that Joseph was a carpenter, but he saw that the man was a hard worker like himself.

Yet rough as they were, Joseph's hands were gentle as they laid the baby in the manger. The ox had never seen a newborn baby before. He stared curiously at the tiny hands waving in the air.

"It is time for us to sleep, Mary," the man said. "The baby will be safe here in the manger."

For the rest of the night the ox watched over the baby Jesus while Mary and Joseph slept. Once the baby stirred and woke. The ox moved close to the manger, and soon the baby slept again, lulled by the steady rhythm of the ox's breathing.

And so began the very first Christmas.

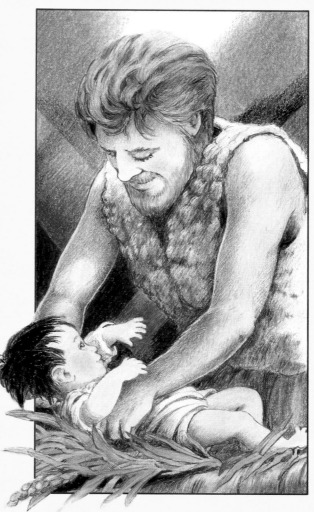

AWAY IN A MANGER

Away in a manger, no crib for a bed,
The little Lord Jesus laid down his sweet head.
The stars in the bright sky looked down where he lay,
The little Lord Jesus asleep on the hay.

The cattle are lowing, the baby awakes,
But little Lord Jesus no crying he makes.
I love thee, Lord Jesus! Look down from the sky,
And stay by my side until morning is nigh.

Be near me, Lord Jesus; I ask thee to stay
Close by me forever, and love me, I pray.
Bless all the dear children in thy tender care,
And fit us for heaven, to live with thee there.

THE ANGEL'S STORY

The stars came out and shone over the stable where baby Jesus lay. All the angels in heaven began to tell the world about the wonderful birth.

But amidst all the joy, someone was crying. It was the smallest angel, who could not join in the music for there was nothing left to play, not even a little hand-drum.

The cherubim and seraphim had given out the instruments: first the trumpets and harps, then the lutes and the flutes, the chime-bars, the violins, the recorders, the cymbals and the triangles; and finally they had given out the little drums and hand-bells. The cherubim and seraphim were immensely tall and had many wings which blazed like fire. The smallest angel thought them very fierce and had not liked to ask them why there was not a single instrument left.

It was the happiest night of the world and all the angels began to sing and play. No one noticed the sad tear-stained face of the smallest angel. As the sound of many voices and instruments swelled, the music seemed to reach across the sky. The smallest angel stopped crying and began to hum. Gradually the hum turned into words and soon a high, clear voice could be heard soaring above the sound of the angel choir; above the fields where shepherds lay watching their sheep; above the stable where the baby had been born.

For though they looked very fierce and had wings that blazed like fire, the cherubim and seraphim had not meant to be unkind. They knew that the smallest angel needed no instrument other than the beautiful voice which sang out the news to the world.

HARK! THE HERALD ANGELS SING

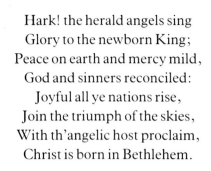

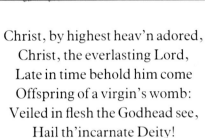

Hark! the herald angels sing
Glory to the newborn King;
Peace on earth and mercy mild,
God and sinners reconciled:
Joyful all ye nations rise,
Join the triumph of the skies,
With th'angelic host proclaim,
Christ is born in Bethlehem.

Hark! the herald angels sing
Glory to the newborn King.

Christ, by highest heav'n adored,
Christ, the everlasting Lord,
Late in time behold him come
Offspring of a virgin's womb:
Veiled in flesh the Godhead see,
Hail th'incarnate Deity!
Pleased as man with man to dwell,
Jesus, our Emmanuel.

chorus

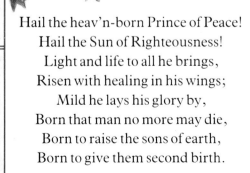

Hail the heav'n-born Prince of Peace!
Hail the Sun of Righteousness!
Light and life to all he brings,
Risen with healing in his wings;
Mild he lays his glory by,
Born that man no more may die,
Born to raise the sons of earth,
Born to give them second birth.

chorus

THE SHEPHERD BOY'S STORY

On the hillside the shepherd boy sat up and rubbed his eyes. The lightning came again, but there was no thunder. The boy watched as the sky grew brighter and brighter. He saw that his father and grandfather were hiding their eyes in terror. He too put up his hands to keep out the light. Then he heard the sound of singing; one voice sang out high above the rest. The shepherd boy peeped between his fingers. In the sky overhead he caught sight of a small face: it was an angel! The boy looked again and now he could see a whole choir of angels. One was taller than the others, with wings that blazed like fire.

"Do not be afraid," the tall angel said. "I bring you good news. Go to Bethlehem and there you will find a newborn baby lying in a manger. The baby's name is Jesus and he is God's gift to you, and to all people on earth."

As the tall angel stopped speaking, the choir began to sing again. The noise was tremendous. Then the light and sound faded. The shepherds found themselves alone on the cold dark hillside, just as before. The boy's grandfather was the first to speak.

"Have I been dreaming?" he asked. "Did I see a bright light and... and..."

"And angels!" whispered the boy. "Yes, grandfather, I saw them too. Can we go to Bethlehem to find the baby as the angel said?"

"And leave our sheep?" said the old man.

"The dogs will keep the sheep safe," said the boy's father. "But we must take presents for the baby. I shall give him a lamb."

"And I shall give him a soft fleece to lie on," said the old man.

The boy was silent. He was sad because he had nothing to give.

As he walked through the darkness, the boy thought about the angel choir and the high voice which sang above the rest. He lifted the reed pipe which hung round his neck, and tried to play the tune the angels sang. But the notes would not come right. "Hush!" said his father. "You will wake the people of Bethlehem with your noise."

The city was quiet when the shepherds arrived, but the innkeeper was already up and sweeping out his yard.

"We are searching for a baby born in a stable and lying in a manger," said the old shepherd.

"You can stop searching then," said the innkeeper. "There's a baby born in my ox's stable this very night."

The shepherds tiptoed into the stable. There they found a young woman wrapped in a blue cloak and a tall man standing beside a manger. A huge ox and a grey donkey peered curiously out of the stall they shared. In the ox's manger a newborn baby lay.

The shepherds knelt down and offered their gifts. The lamb bleated as it was pushed forward.

The shepherd boy lifted the reed pipe to his lips and played the tune the angels sang, with all the notes in the right order. Then he laid the pipe on the hay by the baby's feet.

"This is my gift to the baby Jesus," he said. "Perhaps he will learn to play when he grows up."

WHILE SHEPHERDS WATCHED THEIR FLOCKS

While shepherds watched their flocks by night,
All seated on the ground,
The angel of the Lord came down,
And glory shone around.

"Fear not," said he (for mighty dread
had seized their troubled mind);
"Glad tidings of great joy I bring
To you and all mankind.

"To you in David's town this day,
Is born of David's line
A Saviour, who is Christ the Lord,
And this shall be the sign:

"The heavenly babe you there shall find
To human view displayed,
All meanly wrapped in swathing bands,
And in a manger laid."

Thus spake the Seraph; and forthwith
Appeared a shining throng
Of angels praising God, who thus
Addressed their joyful song:

"All glory be to God on high,
And on the earth be peace;
Goodwill henceforth from heaven to men
Begin and never cease."

THE KINGS' STORY

Many miles from Bethlehem, far away in the East, stood the great palace of King Balthazar. Most days Balthazar was a wise and good king, but today he felt a little foolish. The great jewel from his turban had come loose and fallen into the fishpond. No one could find it.

As night fell, Balthazar was still sitting beside the pond. He sighed. For as long as people could remember, the kings of his country had worn the great diamond. And now it was gone. Balthazar gazed at the pond. Then he looked again. Something was gleaming in the water, something brilliant like a great white jewel. Balthazar leant over and stretched out his hand. But as soon as he touched the water, the gleam broke into a hundred tiny points of light. It was not a jewel he had seen, but a star reflected on the surface of the water.

Balthazar looked up at the sky and saw a star brighter than all the others. It glowed like a lamp and it seemed to call him. Balthazar stood up. He forgot all about the diamond in the pond. Something told him that he must follow the star and it would lead him to where a new king had been born, a baby who would become the king of kings.

Balthazar set off that night, riding on a camel. He took with him a casket of myrrh. As he rode, the star seemed to move ahead to show him the way.

Far beyond the boundaries of his own land, Balthazar met another lonely figure riding through the night. It was King Caspar, who also followed the star. He carried a casket of frankincense.

It took three days to ride through Caspar's great kingdom.

Then the kings found themselves in a strange desert land, and there they met King Melchior, who was an old man with a white beard. A boy rode behind him, carrying a casket of gold.

Twelve days after Jesus had been born, the three kings arrived in Bethlehem. They were surprised when the star led them straight through the city, past the great houses, past the comfortable inn and into a courtyard where a red-faced man was chasing chickens. The star seemed to hover for a moment and then it stopped, directly over the roof of a low, straw-covered barn.

"This stable cannot be the place," said Caspar.

"It is not a fitting place for a king to be born," said old Melchior.

Balthazar remembered the jewel he had lost. "This baby is not an ordinary king," he said. "He does not need palaces or jewels. I know this is the right place."

The three kings entered the stable and knelt down in front of the manger. The baby was lying on a soft fleece. A reed pipe lay at his feet. Somewhere in the darkness a lamb bleated.

Melchior presented his casket of gold. Caspar presented his casket of frankincense. Balthazar bowed his head. "Here is myrrh for the baby born in a stable. The child born to be the king of kings."

When Balthazar returned to his palace, he no longer cared about the lost diamond. He told his people to leave it at the bottom of the pond. For Balthazar had found a far more precious jewel, a baby who would grow up to bring peace and joy to the world.

WE THREE KINGS OF ORIENT ARE

We three kings of Orient are,
Bearing gifts we travel afar –
Field and fountain, moor and mountain,
Following yonder star.

O star of wonder, star of night,
Star with royal beauty bright,
Westward leading, still proceeding,
Guide us to thy perfect light.

Born a King on Bethlehem's plain,
Gold I bring to crown him again:
King for ever, ceasing never,
Over us all to reign.

chorus

Frankincense to offer have I,
Incense owns a deity nigh.
Pray'r and praising, all men raising,
Worship him, God most high.

chorus

Myrrh is mine, its bitter perfume
Breathes a life of gathering gloom;
Sorrowing, sighing, bleeding, dying,
Sealed in a stone-cold tomb.

chorus

Glorious now behold him arise,
King and God and sacrifice;
Alleluia, alleluia,
Praise of him fill the skies!

chorus

O COME, ALL YE FAITHFUL

O come, all ye faithful,
Joyful and triumphant,
O come ye, O come ye to Bethlehem;
Come and behold him
Born the King of Angels:

O come, let us adore him,
O come, let us adore him,
O come, let us adore him,
Christ the Lord!

God of God,
Light of Light,
Lo! he abhors not the Virgin's womb;
Very God,
Begotten not created:

chorus

See how the shepherds,
Summoned to his cradle,
Leaving their flocks, draw nigh with lowly fear;
We too will thither
Bend our joyful footsteps:

chorus

Lo! star-led chieftains,
Magi, Christ adoring,
Offer him incense, gold and myrrh;
We to the Christ Child
Bring our hearts' oblations:

chorus

Child, for us sinners
Poor and in the manger,
Fain we embrace thee, with awe and love;
Who would not love thee,
Loving us so dearly?

chorus

Sing choirs of angels,
Sing in exultation,
Sing, all ye citizens of heav'n above;
Glory to God
in the highest:

chorus

Yea, Lord, we greet thee,
Born this happy morning,
Jesu, to thee be glory giv'n;
Word of the Father,
Now in flesh appearing:

chorus